BY Actors, FOR Actors

A collection of original
MONOLOGUES &
PERFORMANCE
PIECES

Volume 3

Edited by
CATHERINE GAFFIGAN

Excalibur Publishing
New York

Published by:
Excalibur Publishing Inc.
511 Avenue of the Americas, Suite 392
New York, NY 10011

Cover design: Peter J. Byrnes

Library of Congress Cataloging in Publication Data
Gaffigan, Catherine.
    By actors, for actors.

    1. Acting. 2. Monologues. 3. Drama--Collections.
I. Title
PN2088.G34   1991   812'.04508   91-74160
ISBN 0-9627226-2-6 (pbk.) (v. 1)
ISBN 0-9627226-5-0 (pbk.) (v. 2)
ISBN 1-885064-01-2 (pbk.) (v. 3)

Printed in the United States of America

Table of Contents

PERFORMANCE PIECES

Female

Male

INTRODUCTION

When Sharon Good and I conceived the idea of *By Actors, For Actors*, we planned to produce just one volume of monologues based on real-life experiences. But our concept prompted such an enthusiastic response from writers that we were faced with a marvelous dilemma: what to do with the remaining written material. Thus, we produced Volume 2, which was followed by a volume for younger performers called *By Kids, For Kids*.

The inspiration to prepare the subsequent volumes really came from the rich emotional life which our contributing authors have so generously presented. As this volume affirms, the diversity of human experience is astounding: wondrous and appalling. Thanks to the courage and skill of our contributing authors, we have the privilege of making these events available to you so that you may "give them voice."

It is especially gratifying to provide monologues and performance material with a full range of age, ethnicity and emotional "tone." If you feel that you need guidance about either monologue selection or preparation, please refer to the Introduction to Volume 1 of *By Actors, For Actors*, which contains comprehensive basic instructions.

We would be pleased to hear from you regarding your use of these monologues and performance pieces, especially the circumstances in which you performed your selection. You may write to Excalibur Publishing at the address on the copyright page of this book.

We wish you abundant success!

Acknowledgments

My very special thanks to my friend and publisher, Sharon Good, for making our collaboration a delight.

Catherine Gaffigan
New York City, 1995

This book is dedicated to my
brothers, Timothy and James, for
all that we have shared.

Monologues

The Birth Certificate
Anonymous

A couple of months ago, I had a mad urge to get my chart done. My astrological profile. And to get it done, I had to know exactly where I was born and the time. My father had always said to me, "You were born at 7:11," and I took that to mean the time of my birth was 7:11. So I called him to make sure of the time, and he said, "No, you weren't born at 7:11, that was a joke I made about the store. Which birth certificate do you have?" And I said, "I have one that's white, it looks like a mimeo sheet copy." He said, "No, that's the wrong birth certificate." And I like blanked out for a minute, like I saw stars, and I went, "What do you mean, the wrong birth certificate?" And he said, "That's the one I had made up for your mother. She had a hard time dealing with being forty-two when you were born, so we just made one up for the year 1955*, but that's not really the year you were born. I'll send you the certificate from the hospital." And it turned out I was really born in 1952*, not 1955*, so I'm three years older than I thought I was. What a shock! They faked my birth certificate! Isn't that illegal or something! My mother is dead, so I can't find out why she was so worried about being forty-two. I mean, she had a baby, right? All my relatives knew how old she was. My brother knew. They didn't have to lie when he was born, 'cause she was only twenty, so that didn't bother her. She really had an age thing, though. I remember my mother, when we rode on the train saying, "Remember — you're not twelve." And I thought it was so I could ride at half-fare. It's really a shock. I only wanted to have my astrology chart done, and I learned much more than I ever expected. Do you think this makes us a dysfunctional family?

*change year, if needed, to be appropriate for your age

The Regulars
by Marie Moody

Look, I'm really sorry. I never thought he could be married to someone so normal. I mean, we don't think of these guys as human. Try and understand where I'm coming from. Jeffrey was just a customer to me. These guys come in and they fall in love with one of the girls. Sometimes, I mean, they project stuff onto her — you know what I mean — and if a girl is smart, she knows exactly how to play it. I mean, you have to be sort of like a blank slate, and they write you how they want you, and then you have to take on those characteristics. Like, some of the guys want you sweet and troubled, sort of like you just got mixed up with the wrong crowd, and then they think they can save you. But first they want to see if they can trust you, so they start coming in every time you're working, and they say, "I don't care about your dancing. I just want to talk with you. You're different from the others." So a girl would naturally suggest the guy take her into the champagne lounge, where it's more private. Only it's really not, 'cause the whole room is a two-way mirror, and if the management knows a guy is bad news, they come back and check pretty often. I mean, yeah, the guy's paying $300 an hour, but we're not talking about a brothel here, just adult entertainment. They try and find out your real name. That can usually take a couple weeks, depending on how the girl plays it. Once they find that out, they start thinking they have some special connection to you. We refer to them as our regulars. Jeffrey was a regular. I mean, you could try and look at it this way — at least he wasn't having a real affair.

Stress-Free Company
by Katie Clegg

I met a lot of people. I had quite a few conversations with a guy named Earl. We sat in the lounge and watched lots of videos together. I think he probably was a Vietnam vet. Once he went on about bullets in his leg and showed me his scars. He showed a lot of flesh, actually, especially when he'd get up and bend over to work the VCR. Every day he'd wear the same falling-down corduroy pants. Anyway, I didn't ask him flat out about Vietnam, 'cause I thought he might flip on me, so we pretty much stuck to Jay Leno. There were other patients, too. I remember two women who cried a lot and babbled about their kids. But I couldn't really relate. So when Earl wasn't in the lounge, I'd usually go to my room and wait for the nurse to come by with my 'ludes in a Dixie cup.

You know, you're under constant surveillance there. I'm surprised they didn't have minicams mounted on the ceiling. They probably did, hidden somewhere. Every single half hour, a nurse opens your door and peeks in. That's 48 times in a twenty-four hour period. Believe me, it gets old fast. And before you know it, your life regulates into 30-minute intervals. You start timing your bathroom visits between half past and the hour so you're always available. I mean, if you can help it, you don't want the nurse banging on the bathroom door saying, "Hello?" God! One night I thought about tying the curtains into a noose and hanging there for a few minutes just to make rounds less boring for the night staff. Give 'em a good dose of adrenaline, I think. Those nurses actually think they're your friends. The day nurse comes by and introduces herself to you and says things like, "I'll be around if you want to talk later." As if those little chats are casual. They're mandatory. They're also ridiculous. One time a nurse came out with, "But you're so young and pretty to be here." I said, "Oh, you mean you can be too young and pretty to want to die? Well, why didn't someone tell me? I'm sorry. Wow, I must be here under false pretenses. Can I go now?" I think I pissed her off. She just took more notes and said, "Well, if you want to talk later . . ." That's what I liked about Earl — no pressure. You could talk to him about Jay Leno or just take your 'ludes like a good patient and zone with him in front of the TV — completely stress-free. I really miss Earl sometimes.

A Call to the Administrator
by Ramona M. Flores

My mom is getting her gall bladder removed tomorrow at 8:00 AM. She's been very sick.

Today she gives me a call and says, "Oh, Mona, I just got a call from one of the hospital's assistants who called on my doctor's behalf to inquire if I wore contact lenses, corrective lenses or any dental implants. It's hospital policy that someone hold them through surgery," she says. "I don't want to wake up without my teeth and vision." To which I reply, "I understand perfectly, Mom, but the thought of having to carry them around with me is not quite thrilling and, in all honesty, I'm real touchy about things like that." Hey, we all have our idiosyncrasies.

So I call the hospital's main number, and all is confirmed — they would not be responsible for her teeth or glasses. The receptionist was adamant. "No, no, no," she said. "We will not be responsible." At this point, I am fit to be tied. I mean, common sense. What are the odds of someone stealing your teeth, or that they would even fit, and these glasses are not Ray-Ban.

So I call back the hospital's main number, but this time I disguise my voice so I would be connected to the administrator.

"Hello, yes. Is this Montefiore Hospital? My name is Flora from Flowers Forever in Brooklyn. Yes, well, I just spoke to one of your administrators over there in regards to sending an arrangement to one of the assistants. Oh, there's only one administrator. Irma Rosenbloom, that's her. Thank you so much. You're a treasure."

"Yes, Ms. Rosenbloom, my name is Ramona Flores and my mother is scheduled for gall bladder removal tomorrow at 8:00 AM. One of your assistants telephoned her to advise that corrective lenses and dental implants could not be worn during surgery. She said a family member would have to hold onto these personal items, because the hospital would not be responsible for them. Is this true? Don't you have a petty cash box for these kinds of things? I see. Listen, ma'am, my mother is nervous enough about the surgery. Now her vanity is kicking in, and above all, after I escort her to surgery, I have a class to attend, and it perturbs me greatly to carry these things along. If I place these items in a little brown envelope, could you find it in your heart to take them to her after surgery?"

Well, this woman was laughing so hard, I had to hold the phone away from my ear. She said. "I'll do better than that. I'll hold the envelope myself, and I'll see that your mother gets it. It will be there when she wakes up."

So I'm taking bets and giving odds of ten-to-one that the envelope will never appear. Want to bet?

Tia and the Butterflies
by Charlotte Winburn MacArthur

What you have till it's gone is radiation, and what you have afterward is your bone marrow back, if you're lucky. The world behind my cousin Tia's door was photography and radiance and meditation every day. One minute she's out there taking her photos, energetic and smiling, and the next minute, zap! Gilda Radner time — ovarian cancer. Chaos inside Tia's world. Where did it come from? Tia made a joke and said the gypsies brought it.

What you do is go to the hospital, and they put you in a tent and take out your bone marrow and then bombard you with enough radiation to murder an entire army. But all it does is kill what bone marrow they missed and murder! destroy! heavy artillery! nuke! the cancer and oh, so sick you are while they do it and later. And, of course, your hair goes. Everybody knows that.

Tia had gone through her own door and dropped into chaos, where the malignant black cells eat the good ones and no way out. But because it was Tia, there were butterflies there, too. Butterflies and chaos, chaos and butterflies. I saw her in the hospital in the little clear tent where they put her, all her radiance suffocated out of her. Just Tia with hair gone, with marrowless bones, in the dark but for the butterflies. They hold her radiance. They carry her promises.

Before Tia was ill, her photography was just promising to become stunning. "It will be again," we promised her, "your work, stunning," as she smiled and chuckled, our Tia, and walked proud and brave through that plastic partition. And now that's her only world, the only world to her door, and no one goes in, just gloved hands through the vent.

Oh, Tia, are you scared in there, or can you see the butterflies?

The Soul Attracts What It Needs to Grow
by Eileen Herzog-Bazin

Well, he left me again. I don't know why I can't cry. I guess it's because I'm angry, not so much because he's gone, but because he always leaves peacefully but doesn't say why. Maybe I'd feel differently if I could understand it. But he won't reveal the reasons, and I'm left trying to neutralize my feelings.

What he does tell me is that he has nothing against me, and it's his own confusion. He says he doesn't want to be with anyone right now, and he wants to be alone to paint, teach, read his spiritual books, and to take care of his new business. Is it true, or a way to avoid a confrontation? Wasn't our friendship worth more than that? I thought so. Maybe he has a new lover and has returned to his self-renounced homosexual lifestyle. Or perhaps he doesn't even know why.

I know it bothered him that I am not yet legally divorced. The social pressure of being seen with me may have been too much for him. Or the responsibility of being with a woman with two children. Truthfully, I think I'm at fault. I made him responsible for my happiness. I concentrated all my energies on him and expected that would guarantee our future together. I forgot that there are no guarantees.

But I do believe the soul attracts to it what it needs to grow. And I'm convinced that was his purpose in my life. He was there to make me take a good look at myself. And I do want to go on.

I'm getting stronger day by day now. I'm hurting, but now I can stay alone in silence and meditate. I'm healing and getting stronger.

With a little time, I'm sure I'll be able to forget, forgive, and maybe even bless and thank him. After all, his presence in my life was a gift, and his departure an even greater one.

The Funeral (A Fish Story)
by Natalie Shaham

When my children were very young, I took them to Maine during the summer. We rented a place on Panther Pond — down east, as they say. To be more exact, we rented several places — namely, a cooking house, a sleeping house, a boat house and an outhouse. We had what the children called "homemade water," created by pumping a handle up and down while water came out a spout. And we had a kerosene gas stove. One of the things we didn't have was electricity. On the wall of our outhouse was a poster of Queen Victoria. Underneath was inscribed, "To Our Blessed Queen."

Have you ever been in the Maine woods in the rain? In Maine it doesn't matter how warm the summer weather is. If it rains, it's cold. And if you happen to be four little kids and a mother who went to Maine for sunshine and swimming, rain in Maine can be disastrous. The trick is to find some way to keep busy and happy. Ha!

Our rainy day extended itself into a second, then a third, then a fourth day. Then I stopped counting. Each day we all put on slickers and boots, the elder children helping the younger ones, and we would walk to the lake's edge to watch the rain falling dismally into the water.

On one particular day, a dead fish had washed up on the shore. This was a very exciting event. The children examined it at great length — its scales, its shape, its fins, its eyes. What a marvelous thing to find a dead fish on a rainy summer day in Maine! My suggestion that we should have a funeral for the fish was met with great enthusiasm. We took the fish home to prepare. Jack found an old shoebox. Jody lined it with paper towels to make a nice, soft paper towel mattress. Nancy crayoned the shoebox top with flowers and a wreath, and Sally put the top on the box.

Back outside, we began our funeral march. The children each took turns as pallbearer, carrying the box. Jack was first, then Nancy, then Jody. We all marched along the wet paths through the weeds singing *Onward Christian Soldiers, America, Silent Night*, assorted nursery rhymes and any other songs all the children knew. But before Sally's turn came to be pallbearer, our funeral ended abruptly. Jody threw the box on the ground and shouted, "I'm not staying at this funeral! That fish stinks!" The children ran off in all directions, laughing and squealing. Guess who got to play gravedigger?

I Was A Closet Woman
by Chocolate Waters

I cut off my hair and wore a crew cut, like a truck driver, like a marine, like an adolescent boy. I didn't want anyone to find out that I was a closet woman. What if they found out I was a woman? They might make me act like Nancy Reagan, like Marla Maples, like Mary Mother of God. Oh God! I might have to work for 59¢ on the dollar. I might have to bake cherry pies with smiley faces on them. I might have to bleed.

Yes, I was a closet woman. I wore baggy jeans to hide my legs and Army boots to hide my feet. What if they found out I had shapely legs? They might make me cover them with leg warmers, with nylon stockings, with Nair. What if they found out I had women's feet? Some nellie queen might try to put spike heels on them.

I was a closet woman. I wore a black leather jacket to hide my tits. What if they found out I had tits? Some strange baby might try to suck on one. Some weird doctor might try to cut one off. Boys might yell at me on the streets, "Hey, you. You've got — tits!"

I got fat so they wouldn't know I was a woman. I got skinny so they wouldn't know. I became a man. I became a weight lifter so I could be as powerful as a man. I became gay so I could march in a parade. I became outraged because I kept letting "They" define me. I became . . . a woman. I became a woman. I became myself.

It Was Fate
by Selma Kleinman

Janet, stop torturing yourself. I know you think your life is over because Stanley left you. You can't blame yourself, thinking maybe you made him angry. So what if you did?

Listen, I know how you feel, because I've been there, too. Yes, I have.

And not so long ago, either. It was right after I was divorced. I knew I had to go out, to dance, to meet someone, and I'll admit it, I was afraid. And — can you believe this — I was shy.

I decided that the bar at the hotel would be a good place to start. I had my hair done. I remember, it was raining lightly. I parked the car a few blocks away and ran all the way to the hotel. I was so nervous. The rain. My hair. My heart was pounding, my palms were moist. I had to check my hair in the ladies' room. I saw the urinals and I ran out. Oh, my God! I knew I had to calm down, so I found the bar — they called it a lounge, right? And there he was. He listened quietly while I babbled on. He offered me a drink. I needed a drink, so I accepted. It was him. Louis. We sat and spoke for hours. He made me laugh. He told me he was newly separated. He was like a hippie. He was my age, but his hair was long. Charming, of course, witty. He listened, and he drank a bit. I never knew a man like him. He was different. Before I was married, I'd always gone out with students.

That evening was the start of our romance. He was everything I had been warned about. "He's a bum. He's no good." But I found him exciting. I had never felt so wanted. Well, anyway, I wanted. I had never felt so needed; I know now that he saw how needy I was. Whatever it was, we clicked. He was romantic and devilish, and I just became addicted to him. Needing him, wanting him. People said, "Look for the future," but Louis was the now.

We spent so much time together, every possible minute. I think I said something, like "Let's move in together," and he immediately backed off and then backed out of my life completely. He disappeared. Quite suddenly, I was alone again, just like you are now, Janet.

Even now, sometimes, at night when I can't sleep, I think of Louis. I still do, you know. I think of those sweet days when my only thought was, "When would I see him again? When would I kiss him again? When would I love him again?" And I guess a part of me always will. But I see how far I've come. And I know that my time with Louis was really just a kind of intermission. Try to look at it that way, Janet. I know you're hurting, but something better waits for you.

.

New York Autumn
from *Horrible Essays*
by Francine M. Storey

I just felt that I had to talk to you. I feel so desolate . . . so useless . . . so battered . . . so filled with the burden of living in the same place for years and making all kinds of futile efforts to become successful and self-sustaining, and it hit me big the other night when I went down to the Village. There it was — almost exactly as it had been in 1963. A chilled autumn evening. Young people in long scarves rushing around to book stores, movies and restaurants, and they all looked as if they were the answer to the world. It was just as it had been, except in 1963, we were those young people, going to the Waverly, eating at Emilio's. How is it possible that people evaporate, but buildings remain?

The only really new thing is the McDonald's on West 3rd Street. Otherwise, very little has changed, except that no one was there except me, and I felt like I had died. Where was the small blonde girl who was 22 and looked 15? Where was the good-looking Italian boy who said he was going to win an Academy Award? Where was the tall boy from St. Louis who liked to take pictures? Where was the brunette girl who scribbled in notebooks? Gone, totally gone. I was the dead person sent back to walk the streets — a spirit without a burial. There are no headbands or love beads here. The hair is cut jagged and dyed fuchsia, and the clothes are funny. But, after all, fashion makes no difference. What is always in Greenwich Village is the surge of youth and new beginnings. The beginning of a new art movement. A new film trend. A new and very unusual piece of choreography. The theatres are still there. The cafes are still there. And my first apartment in New York City is still there on Bleecker and Sullivan. And it was there, in the shower of that apartment, that I first tried to kill myself, because I couldn't make someone love me. And that is what I have spent my life doing — trying to make men love me.

Have We Found Each Other?
by Laton Carter

In your own sweet way, you tell me about your VW bus. It's an omen, you say. Ever since you got it. When it started to rain, all the seals leaked. Don't get one, you say. I still want one, I say. I bought it for 1200 and I've put in 2000, you say and smile. I smile, too, and don't find too much to add. I lean against the counter by the hot chocolate machine, and you're by the ice tea dispenser. If I want to find you, I always go to the hot chocolate machine. There you are next to it by the ice tea dispenser, folding napkins. I get a cup of hot chocolate. I stay a while. Then I go out of the kitchen and back on the floor, while you stay in the kitchen folding napkins, waiting for your next order to ring in over the phone, while I think of your face when I go around pouring coffee for everyone. You take your orders out, and I clear the tables, and later in the dishroom, you show me a two-dollar bill you got for your tip. It has the name and address of one of your high school friends written on it. I haven't seen this friend for years, you say. That's another omen, I say.

Of Course They Called It A Tragedy
by Gus Edwards

They were searching for a killer, they said. Sure they were. That's exactly who they were eager to find, right? The man who killed the man they were all calling "The Enemy of America." Forget that he had whites following him and agreeing with what it was he was preaching. Forget that he had won the Nobel Prize for Peace. Forget that he said, "I have a dream that is deeply rooted in the American dream." Those things were only making them hate him more.

Do they seriously want me to believe that the FBI wasn't secretly happy when they heard that he had been shot? That J. Edgar Hoover, that great defender of American democracy, wasn't in some room laughing his head off when he got the news? And that many folks all over the North and South wasn't holding secret parties because this thorn in their side had been removed in the most effective way a person can be removed. With a bullet in the face.

Of course they called it a tragedy. And of course they were looking for the man who pulled the trigger. They were searching the cities and scouring the countryside with every resource they had. And with one prayer in their hearts: "Oh, God, don't let it be a white man. Let it be one of their own." Some eye-rolling, rabid-looking black loony spouting quotes from Nietzsche and the Koran while waving a pistol in the air. He would, of course, have to be subdued with about 30 bullets through the heart. Then all would be right with America once more.

They had gotten lucky with Malcolm. It was black men who had done the deed. And perhaps this time, if they prayed hard enough, maybe, just maybe, lightning might strike twice in the same spot.

0600 Hours
by Marsh Cassady

Most days it was hot enough to feel the heat right through the soles of my black regulation shoes. But I didn't care. I'd been accepted for cadet training, and that's all that mattered. I'd passed the tests and was going to fly. Me, who'd never even been close to a plane until the last couple of months.

I hadn't been up yet. That would come later. But I'd taken my basic training and I loved it. Not everything I had to put up with — half of it KP, up at 0230, scrubbing pots and pans — but just being alive on God's earth. A different part of the earth than I'd ever expected to see. Rock-studded mountains so high I had to throw back my head to see to the snow-covered tops. And air not choked with fumes from steel mill stacks or burning slag heaps, but clear and pure.

I loved Colorado and was sorry to leave. Yet the only thing that mattered was that I'd passed all the tests, physical and mental. Passed with flying colors. So I was sent to Minter Field*, a pre-cadet, waiting for an opening to begin my pilot's training.

I didn't understand why I wanted that so badly. Up to then I'd been earthbound; my only acquaintance with planes was watching from the ground.

One morning after I dressed, I looked outside. It was 0600 and already hot. Minter Field* was part of a giant bowl where heat and air pollution seemed to lie like smoke in a bottle. Yet it was beautiful country, too, with groves of orange and lemon trees and vast fields of potatoes.

And any day now there were bound to be some openings. That's why I felt like whistling or praising God or both on my way to morning formation. We stopped outside the mess hall for "an important announcement."

Major Reynolds stood before us, a fat little man with red hair and freckles. He looked from face to face, and then glanced down at a sheet of paper he held, then up again. I wondered what was going on.

Let me tell you, I found out. I felt my knees sag and my face grow hot and my throat become thick. I thought it was a joke, some kind of sick joke. There wouldn't be any pilot training. Not for me nor the others. We were washed out. "At the convenience of the government." Some stupid asshole decided we were needed elsewhere. So to hell with our tests, our records, our hopes.

When Reynolds finished, it was quiet, absolute silence. Then they started to sing. "Off we go into the wild blue yonder, flying high." Well, I didn't want any part in that crap. No, sir.

We came to another group of cadets, real ones, men who would go on to be pilots. They were hanging out their barracks windows. "Boo hoo! Can't be a pilot," they yelled. "Go home to mama! Boo hoo!" I wanted to kill the sons-of-bitches. If I ever caught one of them alone, I thought to myself, I'd beat the shit out of him. Screw the pretense of holding your head up high. Screw the Air Corps* and the idiots who decided to wash us out.

*Younger men may substitute "Lackland Air Force Base" and "Air Force."

Maybe It's A Club Act
by Armand A. Ruhlman III

They took over the building next to me. The cops. Whole bunch of them charged into this old abandoned wreck. Like commandos. Like one of those Hollywood movies. Yeah, where cars blow up and women get pulverized. Like one of those SWAT teams. Maybe it's a club act. That's what it looked like. Squatters. They got some squatters. Couple of homeless dudes. Threw them out. Into the street. Right smack dab on the sidewalk. Total darkness. Middle of the night. Bummer, huh?

Then I had this dream. Did I tell you the dream? Yeah, the creature dream. The robot dream. Where this crazy flipped-out doctor dude creates this thing. Puts together a female creature who can walk and talk. Move and groove. Laugh and cry. The works. Can do anything and everything a human can do, but it's not human. She's not human. It's a female robot. Sleek and sassy. Ready for action. Any kind of action. But on the inside it's all components. Yeah, wires, circuits. Millions of little tiny video screens. Weird stuff like that. She's programmed, this robot chick. Zapped how to think. How to act. How to get up, down and all around.

They said they wanted to talk to me so I wouldn't end up on the sidewalk, too. All by myself, somewhere in some dark alley. Some freaky flophouse. It could take a while. Yeah, they said it's going to be a slow, painful thing. They said you won't even recognize me. At the end. They said I'm going to crumble into nothing. The life drained out of me. Hardly able to move, breathe. Hardly able to do much of anything. Except lie there. I don't want to just lie there. I don't want to be old, man. I don't want to shrivel up into some thing. Some thing somewhere in some dark horrible place. I asked them about vitamins. And minerals. Nutrition. Herbs. To heal.

My body. To get well. Plants, roots, flowers. That's where herbs come from. The earth. The ground. Mother earth. They looked at me funny. Mean funny. Not nice funny. Yeah, like I was a witch or something. Like they wanted to set fire to me. Burn me at the stake. Right there in the middle of all the sick, dying people who were being killed by pills and gizmos and gadgets. Burn me like I was some kind of heretic. You know, the cats and chicks who were rebels. Who rebelled against those old farts who ran things. Back in the middle ages. Remember the middle ages? The inquisition. Yeah, torture and killing of heretics, especially women. They were really big on burning women to death. For weeds. For eating and cooking weeds. To get well. That's why they were killed. For loving weeds instead of Jesus Christ.

I told them to rot. 'Cause they said I was going to rot. They said my bones would kind of melt. My face would get gray and clammy. I don't want my face to get clammy. I don't like clams. I like my face. Don't you like my face? Tell me you like my face. It's a scream thing I've got. A psychic scream. From inside. Inside my atoms. My atoms are screaming. Yeah, I can feel it. My atoms are unhappy about something. That's what I think. That's why I got this thing.

Raphael
by Brother Augustine Towey, CM

Emily. Emily. Doesn't answer. Doesn't care. Doesn't want to. Doesn't have to. Never was fast on her feet — never had to be. Little spoiled, little lazy. Little lady. She'd rather sit and talk. Emily. Pass the time. Southern belle. Ah, well. Somewhere now — someplace, not here — holding court. I call. I call. Wait. Listen. I listened to the chatter down the hall. Wouldn't know what to say to a lady anyhow. Bow. Straighten. Keep eyes down. Keep hands out of pockets. Don't shuffle. Don't cough. Keep your wits about you, you idiot. Overheard. Her voice above the others. Could tell her voice in a hundred, over the crowd. Wind chimes, was it? Doesn't do it justice. The others listened, didn't hear. I heard. Noticed, paid attention. Lotta good it did me. Well . . . patience. Emily. Never too late. Never too early either. What's late? 50 years? 51 years is late. I'm early. I'll tell her Monday, give her a call. No, barge in, through the front door, bang into the parlor, turn her by the shoulders, plant one on her mouth. She'll know. I'm fierce as steel when my mind's made up. Her house for parties. The banister covered with ropes made of leaves, colored paper strung from the lights, silk dresses that make that whooshing noise, lace on bare shoulders. Her little feet scurried over the parquet, serving punch, inviting others to a corner, whispering, whispering. I should have said something, spoken myself. What the hell good is listening. Wallflower, bump on a log. Walking with her once, fell down the stairs, gaping at her. Bump on my head, bruise on my ass. All for the little lass, the little lady. Could've been worse. Who's to say? Could've been . . . could've been . . . ah, well . . .

I Looked At Her and I Could Not Move
by Laton Carter

We were in the parking lot of the grocery store. It was raining and all the windows were fogged. She worked the key another time and then we gave up. We got out and she locked the doors. The rain bounced on our shoulders. She said she would have to call her dad. We stood for a moment and then started to walk back, the water making small lights on the asphalt under the street lamps. She wore a black pork pie hat, a double-breasted jacket and a denim skirt that went past her knees. I didn't even look at her and I could feel everything — her eyes and hair under the hat, her skirt brushing against my pant leg. We went past an all-night store and I said to wait a minute. I went in and bought two chocolate bars and came out. She asked me what I had, and I said that I didn't have anything, and we started to walk again.

The cold set in and we tried to walk faster, and she told me about where she'd lived. That she'd moved from Connecticut to Texas when she was six. That even though she'd lived most of her life in Texas, Connecticut was still clear to her. I asked her what she considered home, and she said she didn't know, that she had never felt a part of Texas, but that Connecticut was too long ago to be a home. I started to talk about Oregon, but I stopped, because we had made it back to my place. I unlocked the door and let her into my room. She sat on the couch and I went to make coffee. In the kitchen, I looked out the window while the hot water went through the grinds. Orange and yellow leaves from the tree in the courtyard had stuck to the glass. I looked over my shoulder at her. She was bent over hugging her knees. She said she was cold. I looked at her, her chin touching her knees, her hair connecting with her wet skirt. In that moment I felt some instinct, some sort of conjugal force. I wanted to protect her and keep her warm.

I poured the coffee and walked over and handed it to her. She took it with both hands and held it under her mouth. I went to my dresser, pulled out a drawer and took out two pairs of socks. I came back and sat down on the carpet. She had leather slip-on shoes and no socks. I took her wet shoes off and held her left foot between my hands. It was cold and white, and I rubbed my hands over it, working the warmth back in. She watched as I put a cotton sock over her foot and then a wool one. I did the same with her right foot and afterward rubbed both feet between my hands. Then I went to get myself a coffee. She kept her head down, looking at her feet, the steam from her cup gently rising. I came back and sat down by her. She said she was starting to get the feeling back in her feet, and she wiggled her toes under the socks. We both looked at her feet, and then I got up to get the chocolate bars. They were on the counter next to the sink. As I walked over to them, I tried to think of something to say. I picked them up and turned around and looked at her, but there was nothing. I looked at her, and I could not move. If there was anything, I thought, something I could say.

White Light
by Joe Miserendino

I thought that maybe I'd say a prayer, you know, but then, I was never the type for that. You have to be the type for that, and I never really was. I always believed that praying was as universally meaningful as using a coaster at a cocktail party — a nice gesture, but, you know, easily dismissed. Praying is organized wishing, but because of the tradition behind it, it's permissible. Wishing is for fools, I was always told, but praying is good and will be rewarded. Sorry, but there's just no way I could believe that.

Anyway, that is what I was thinking about as I was sitting at my desk in my tiny studio apartment. I was in one of those moods where my face goes blank and I gaze into the triangular patterns of my wallpaper, which, during these moods, start to look like spider webs.

I remembered a dream that I had a few nights earlier. I was in a pitch black movie theater, and I was looking for someone I knew, or waiting for someone to call out my name, or gesture, or anything, but no one ever did, and so I kept wandering around the aisles until the movie ended and the lights came on. Everyone had suddenly vanished. I remember gazing into the blinding whiteness of the screen, and the dream faded. And when I woke up, I realized how alone I really was and how much I hated it.

Today, I met a woman, one of our new employees, and we smiled at each other for what I thought were a few seconds longer than needed. But immediately I thought it was one of those "Yes, I think you're very attractive, too, but there is no way in hell we are ever going to be together, so why are we smiling at each other?" smiles. And with that, we exchanged pleasantries, and I went back to my desk and sat down.

But as it got closer and closer to lunch time, it struck me that it was as easy for two people to get together as it was for two shadows to intersect on a sidewalk at midday. At five minutes to twelve, I strode over to her desk and asked her to lunch, and that's how it began.

I had spent too long staring into those patterns on the wallpaper in my apartment, so long that they had become webs in which I'd been caught. Unable to move, and just waiting. It took about twenty minutes to tear the wallpaper off the walls, and the painting took me an hour and a half. And now the walls are sparkling white, but not a white that blinds. It is a white of possibilities.

The Outsider
by Gus Edwards

I hate this city, I really do. It ain't bad enough that it deprives you of everything but the bare necessities of life, but it also got to show you what it is you're being deprived of. So if you can't afford a car (which, of course, don't make sense in this city, since there ain't no place to park), it's wall-to-wall cars wherever you look. Mercedes, Ferraris, Porsches, BMW's, fantail Caddies and every kind of sportscar you can imagine. All of them shiny, buffed up and new. All of them with some pretty girl with long hair who you would kill your parents for, sitting in the front seat next to the driver. One more way for this city to tell you, "Some got it, but you don't, loser."

Or if you live in a hovel, as I do. Then it's all these glassed-in doorways where women with their dogs walk in and out, while doormen in gloves and uniforms touch their hats and open the doors for them, as if them women couldn't open the doors for themselves.

It's hell being out here on the street, but I ain't got no place else to go.

The place where I live, everybody there is like me. Broke, depressed, down all the time. Everybody got a job. None of us is criminal or anything like that. But after the rent is paid and money is took out for food, there ain't that much left for any kind of luxury. So those of us who don't hang out in bars stay home and watch TV night after night, till it's time to go to sleep. If you watch TV on any kind of regular basis, you know how much fun that got to be. Boring, boring, boring.

Weekend like this, sitting around the house is more than dull. It's deadly. So I walk down the street looking at all the things I hate this city for. I look at the fine clothes in store windows. I look at the fine women walking up and down the streets. I look in on all the nice restaurants I can't afford to go into. Look at all the fine stereos and TV's and VCR's in the showcases. And dream of a time when all of that'll change.

This is the delight and the pain of living in this city. I love it and I hate it. But most of all, I just want to belong. I just want it to love me like I love it. Now, I want to know, is that too much to ask?

Snakes
by Gus Edwards

I don't like snakes. Never had and never will, it's as simple as that. I don't see any reason why they on the planet. I know there must be a reason, but I can't see it.

People I know tell me it's ridiculous to be afraid o' snakes. But I can't help myself, I been that way ever since I was a kid. People show me a snake, dead or alive — I don't care — and I'm gone from that spot. Gone from the area completely.

When I was in the Army, guys used to put dead snakes in my bed just to see me jump a mile. One day I caught a fellow doing it, when I try to put my fist through his face. Then people knowed I was serious about not liking snakes.

This last woman I was going out with — Brenda — she had a snake for a pet. A python named Archie. You ever hear stuff like that? Naming a snake as though it was human. Said it was her lucky charm. Used to wear it around her shoulders, talking to it and showing it to people. Thing was huge — not poisonous, but huge — but I didn't like it. So I told her up front, "Look, me and snakes don't get along. Truth is, I am afraid o' them, and I can't stand for them to be near me. But you like the snake, he's your pet and everything like that, so I ain't going to say nothing. Just keep that thing outta my way, and the world will be fine."

And she did. At least for awhile. A long while. Then one night late, after we came from dinner and having a few drinks, we was lying out in bed with the lights off, talking and listening to music on the radio. That kind of quiet time in the city when you can't even hear traffic anymore. I was kinda falling asleep when I feel this lump move. I turn and it was the goddamn snake trying to work its way under my arm. Goddamn! Goddamn! It musta got outta the cage. Jesus Christ, I didn't know what to do. I jump outta that bed and run to the bathroom, because to tell the truth, I was about to pee myself from fright.

When I come out, Brenda sitting up with the lights on, petting that thing and talking to it. "Oh, Archie, why you scare Willie like that? How'd you get outta your cage anyway, you bad boy."

I couldn't believe that. My heart is pounding and that woman is petting her snake. But I didn't want to say anything either. So I just got my clothes from the other room, put them on and left. I don't know if she even realize I was gone. That's how busy she was talking to that snake.

I never went back and she never call. So that was it. A nice situation broken up all because of a goddamn snake.

See, I don't believe it was an accident that it was a snake who messed up the scene in the Garden of Eden. I mean, the place was paradise. Adam and Eve had everything good till that snake come in to spoil it. Now, for you and I to see paradise, we got to die first. Why? All because of a goddamned snake. No. I don't want to see another one. Ever.

A Word from Jack
by Francine M. Storey

When I first started dating, my mother told me to behave as if I was nature's nobleman. Boy, that didn't work. I wasn't getting kissed or anything else, not even when I took out Myra, the town punchboard. Every guy in town was getting into her pants except me. Something had to change, so I had this serious talk with my dad, and he said to me, "Son, treat a lady like a whore and a whore like a lady." I've fucked a lot of whores and I've treated them like ladies, and I fucked a lot of ladies and I've treated them like whores, and it always worked. Always. Except it's not working anymore, especially at the gym.

I used to do real well at gyms. I'd hit the Nautilus machines around 11 AM on a Saturday morning, and I'd pick out some chick in a skimpy outfit and come onto her real rough and tough. Right off, I'd tell her how great her tits looked and how firm her thighs looked and all that B.S. And within two hours tops, I'd have her in my apartment in bed. But lately these little bitches have been giving me the cold shoulder. Last Saturday, I went to the weight room at my usual time, and I spotted this very sexy brunette pumping iron in a bright pink skin-tight body suit. Boy, I took one look at her and my socks started rolling up and down. So I began chattin' to her, introduced myself real politely and said that she had the most gorgeous gams I'd ever seen in my entire life. And she said, "Thanks for the compliment." Then I suggested that we dispense with the formalities, grab a cab, go to my apartment and have a really good fuck. Do you know what she said? She said, "Scram, Gramps!"

I guess she thought I was old. Hell, I'm only 48. Right then and there, I decided that as soon as I could get $7000 together, I was going to get a facelift, 'cause these chicks seem to be going for the mirror image. They want pretty boys with pretty pusses like those fags who model for Ralph Lauren. Well, I know what I got, and from the neck down, I'm in very good shape. You might even say, fightin' shape. My sister keeps saying to me, "Jack, accept it, you're getting old," and I told her point blank that my equipment is still working fine, and those young broads don't know what they're missing, if they'd only give me a chance.

The Dazzler
by Frank Biancamano

The last time my father and I went to a baseball game together, I was in my early twenties. It was a night game, a year or two before the Dodgers left Brooklyn forever. My father grew up in an age when men wore suit, tie and felt hat to go to a ball game. As many times as we'd been to games together since I was seven or so, his dressing that way for a ball game always astonished me.

It was a warm June evening, with a feel it might get comfortably cool about the fourth or fifth inning and, if we were lucky, turn out to be a game we'd remember. There was a sort of show to keep the crowd occupied until game time. Half dozen ball players from a long-gone generation were introduced. Each sheepishly stepped up to a microphone at home plate and, depending on how frightened they were of microphones, either whispered or shouted "hello" to the crowd. When the name Dazzy Vance blared over the public address system, my father got to his feet and stared hard to get a good look at the man shuffling up to the microphone. Dazzy Vance had pitched for the Dodgers in their hopeless decades between the wars and was, according to my father, the best pitcher Brooklyn ever had and maybe was ever going to have. When he whispered something I couldn't hear into the microphone, my father sighed, "The Dazzler." In that moment, I got to see what my father looked like at twenty. A baseball hero can be what the spirit needs.

My father is the son of immigrant parents. He was just old enough to volunteer for Army service in World War I. In 1924 when Dazzy Vance was creating a legend, my father was getting used to the idea that the large number of sons and daughters of immigrants was given as reason to close the door on immigration from certain countries. At the same time, he might have been living a bewildered agony over what was happening to Sacco and Vanzetti — I can't be sure. I do know when I got to be aware of things and Sacco and Vanzetti were mentioned, his face got a hard set, and you could see in his eyes the subject had to be changed. Somehow, over time, I got the idea my father must have gotten his heroes and his hurts in his young manhood, pretty much as I'd gotten mine in my young manhood.

Performance Pieces

Jilly Rose
from *Flying Through the Sky*
by S. Heide Arbitter

In those days, I stood inside the paintings. I don't know how this worked, exactly, but I'd enter father's studio, from the back, where I'd watch him add color to canvas, then all of a sudden, I'd be smiling at him, looking out through his paintings.

Throughout the gray hours of my school days, I buried myself in my studies. My real love was the studio, but whenever I showed my father my own attempt at art, he'd look at it, cast his eyes to the floor, and whistle. This whistling sound had a soothing effect, though I shouldn't have been lulled by it. I spent many days trying to imitate it, but my pitch being off I never could. The more I tried, the more I failed, the more my heart-felt yearning increased. I'd awake in the morning, grinding my teeth, my knuckles clenched white from frustration. Sometimes, I'd wet the bed. Mother beat me, but I couldn't control myself, and this led to the punishments, that eventually led to my salvation.

Mother was fond of locking me in a closet. She learned it from her mother, she said. I'd sit in the black space for hours, trying to sound the right whistle. To me it was a love call, something that I imagined it to be, because it was disapproval that father was whistling and not the golden call of relationship. One day I hit it, the vibration that carried me out. It started as a low hum, somewhere in the area of my navel, and continued upward, becoming a lively and persistent MMMMMMMMMMM somewhere within the cavity between the temples of my head. One afternoon I took my clothes off in the hot, stuffy closet and rolled myself in toilet paper from head to foot. This made the MMMMMMMMMM more rhythmic, and I sat for hours,

41

swaying back and forth in the closet.

When father died I got my own small apartment and a job as a secretary. This was a mistake, since I wasn't a good typist, and my despair was great. I worked for a lawyer, who was unhappily married. That's why he gave me the job. Daily I sat in my beige cubicle. Sometimes I typed his personal correspondence. Sometimes a couple of bills. I led a secluded existence. I grew to hate everything about the law. It was at this point that my father's face appeared as the typing keys that chained my fingers. I began arriving late each morning. Instead of working, I'd stare at my father's face in the typewriter. "How'd you get there?" I'd whisper. "Is it the same way I entered the paintings?"

Most suicides occur at work. Each afternoon I ate my brown rice, hoping to bite into poison. "You're too thin," the boss commented as he handed me yet another letter to be typed and mailed to his mistress. By then his wife was suing him for divorce. It was freezing in the office. I don't know why, but every time it snowed, the boiler broke, causing me to type with my gloves on, and so evolved my lonely romance with death. Clients phoned the boss while he was at lunch. I didn't answer the phone, and when I did, I'd hiss, "I don't have a lover! Death is my lover!" I assume that the boss, growing tired of his mistress, had plans for me, because he continued to keep me around.

On Christmas Eve, my suspicions were confirmed. I wasn't invited to any parties, so I sat at my desk, tapping the face of my father. The boss sat at his desk, drinking straight from a bottle of bourbon. He offered me a shot, but I said, "no." "You look beautiful tonight," he slurred. "Thank you," I said.

At 11 PM, he came out of his office, bottle in hand. "Why are you still here on Christmas Eve?" he asked. "I have no other place to go." I knew I made a mistake. The boss shoved the bottle in my face. "Drink up, we're going to party!" "No!" I said, staring into the face of father. "Come on," he said, rubbing the bottle down my arm. "I do have to leave, after all," I said, but he was standing behind me, blocking my way. "Why don't you type me a letter?" "Very well, sir." "Dear Jilly Rose, Merry Christmas, Happy New Year." The boss lunged at me, smashing the bottle over my hands on the face of father in the typewriter. Blood spilled on the keys, but the boss didn't mind. He grabbed me. I caught a piece of glass and scratched his face. He yelled and let go long enough for me to push out from my desk, but I couldn't make the door. He came toward me, "Relax, this won't hurt one bit." He shoved me against the wall, and I began humming in my navel MMMMMMMMM. "You're so pretty," he said from his level of intoxication. He ran his hand down the front of my blouse, ripping it open. "Leave me alone!" I begged, as I inched my way along the wall. Kicking out my leg, I tripped him.

The door wasn't within reach, but the window was. I pulled it open and climbed to the edge. It was cold. "Death take me!" I muttered as I jumped.

I awoke in this room, encased in bandages. At first I thought I'd fallen asleep in the closet, and that mother had awakened me, but then I realized I couldn't move. Although my vision was dark and blurry, I saw that Lothgar was sitting on my toe. He soon began to grow bigger.

The Harmon Killebrew
by Alan Stolzer

Now, I have some books, and I have some earrings. I have anything you want, but you're the one who has to speak up. 'Cause no matter how insightful I am — and I am insightful — I've yet to make a sale to you.

Don't be shy and don't be bashful. Come closer and inspect my wares. Trinkets, flower seeds, various forms and types of clothing. I had incense before most people knew what it was. I see you looking at my assortment of pottery. But don't touch the merchandise unless you ask me first, as I'd be forced to call on Mr. Harmon Killebrew here [*waving bat*] to settle up.

Mr. Killebrew is not for sale. I repeat, not for sale. He is my main source of protection in this most dubious of worlds, and I guarantee any evildoer harboring the slightest evildoing will have Mr. Killebrew's autograph tattooed across his forehead — for life, if he's not careful. Yessir. I have done it before and will do it again if I have to.

Both hands off the harmonicas, young man, or next time we will strike without warning. As I was saying, everything you see's for sale. And all prices are negotiable. Trouble with most people is lack of flexibility. You won't find that the case with me. I could be here today and one thousand miles away tomorrow, with a whole new line of goods. It's not hard, if you're flexible. That's what keeps me going, in case you hadn't noticed.

Do you believe I'm 85? Do you believe I'm 75? Anyone can choose a number, but what I'm trying to say — and pay attention — is, it don't matter, 'cause it's none of your damn business. If I were to release information like that, why, my career would be jeopardized faster than Harmon here could crush a fastball. And Harmon could hit, make no mistake about it. Why, he was one of the greatest righthanded sluggers of all time, that's all.

Harmon Killebrew? Shoot. When Mr. K came striding up to the plate, he didn't make a big show of it. No, sir. He was stocky, see. Kind of purposeful, head down, all business. But when he looked up, it was every man for himself. Then he cocked his namesake like this — a wide, slightly open stance — and didn't move an eyelash. Pure, unadulterated, midwestern American menace, I'm tellin' ya. Oh, that man about sent me to heaven when he rode one into the left field bleachers. Thrills? Honey, you had better not have been within fifty feet of me when he hit one out, 'cause I was letting the world know all about it, in case it already didn't. Not too many people got to me like Mr. K did. No, sir.

I'm not sleepin' here, young man. I warned you already. That there harmonica is now two dollars and seventy-five cents instead of two fifty. I'll teach these young puppies a thing or two about sellin'. Yes, I will. Just because I look away one thousandth of a second, they think I'm fair game. Shoot. I was selling goods long before the poor creature who brought that punk into the world was born. Now where was I? Oh, yes, Mr. K and his personal reign of terror. Used to give me reassurance — that's right, reassurance — to see someone conduct himself as he did. Didn't need nobody. Speak softly and carry the biggest stick you can find. Stands to reason, don't it? Now, I like you. You listen and don't jabber away or try to get my prices down, although I do wonder about that. So, me and Harmon'll do what we can with you. Does jasmine strike your fancy? Here's some nice amulets, or are you more practical-minded today? How about this good wool workshirt, from L.L. Bean? Only slightly used. In very good condition. It's my last offer of the day.

The Duke of Iowa City
by Tessie Ollie Carr

They tell me I was born in Lone Tree, Iowa in 1897, but the first place I remember living in was Wellman, Iowa. I'm the second youngest of seven, and I was spoiled until my sister Elizabeth was born. That house in Wellman was small. We had a fourteen-room house later on. But in Wellman, my father worked hard at carpentry work to keep us fed and clothed, and we were alright.

One thing we never got tired of was Mama and Papa telling of the time they spent on a claim in Dighton, Kansas — of the Indians, rattlesnakes, blizzards, grasshoppers and hunger, because they couldn't raise enough to eat.

When we moved to Iowa City, our lives were completely changed. It was such a big city, we couldn't roam much. No more going to the timber to pick wild flowers and walnuts, hickory nuts, butternuts and hazelnuts.

We had a hound dog named Duke that took us to school every day and waited across the street until we were all in the building. And then he went home and walked my sister Zetta to her work, and he waited outside until all the girl clerks were inside. He didn't care if the men weren't in yet. Then Duke would go home until noon and then bring us all home for lunch, and then take us back again at one o'clock. Sometimes we would see him across the street watching us at recess. He never came in the schoolyard. If one of us couldn't go to school, he would take the rest and then go home and cry until Mother would tell him it was alright.

Duke, to us, was a hero. He was an outdoor dog, as Mother didn't believe in letting a dog in the house. One day after school was out, Zena, a little girl up the block, came to play with us. She was jumping rope on the walk. Duke was on the front steps with me. When Zena stopped, she came on a run and set down on the step right on Duke's tail. He yelped and bit her in the face. He had never bitten any one before, and I think it scared him as bad as it did us. Mother called the doctor who roomed upstairs, and he came down and looked at Zena's face. He said Duke's tooth had just scratched her cheek enough to make it bleed. Papa carried her home and told her he would have Duke killed. But the doctor said not to kill him, because he knew the kind of dog he was. The doctor told Papa just to tie Duke up for a couple of weeks to be sure he wasn't sick. Duke had never been tied before and his heart was about broken. We kids were told to stay away from him, but as the folks were so busy, we just about lived with him during those two weeks to let him know we loved him.

Late that summer, I had rheumatism and was in bed for three weeks. I couldn't even turn over by myself. I know now it was rheumatic fever, as several doctors have told me at sometime in my life I have had it, but they didn't call it that in those days. When school started, I couldn't go, and Duke would take the rest to school and then come back and cry until Mother finally let him in just for a few minutes to see me, and then he would be alright. He was just an all-brown coon dog with a big heart and just as smart. Why, he took train trips by himself.

Whenever my brother Clem had time or could slip away, he would take Duke with him and go to the Black Hills and hunt. They had to go on the Interurban train as far as they could and then walk the rest of the way. Duke refused to sit on the floor, but instead sat on the seat next to Clem, so Clem had to pay the same for him, as he took up a seat. A couple of times a week, Duke would make the trip by himself (without Clem knowing it), and the conductor would keep track, and Clem would pay later for those trips Duke took by himself.

Then we moved to Iowa City, and it was about that time that our bad luck started. Papa's health was getting worse all the time, and the doctor told him if he wanted to live, he would have to go to a warmer climate. Papa decided on Plainview, Texas, where his sister was living. So we packed up and left on the train. But Duke didn't take that train ride with us. That last winter we were in Iowa City, Duke got real sick and died.

And Texas? Well, it was typhoid and a small house and cowboys. I married one of those cowboys, by name of Harry G. Thompson. He fell off his horse one late night when he was riding across our yard. But that's another story.

The White Man's Guide to Rikers Island
by Richard Roy

I was born this really white guy. Upper middle class family. House on a golf course. Across the street was a lake surrounded by mountains.

After my first few minutes arriving here at Rikers Island, I finally understood what the word "minority" meant. I also had no idea what anybody was talking about. It took me a whole month to get familiar with the language. Now at least I have the vocabulary.

Jail was as foreign to me as the North Pole. To relieve my initial boredom, I took up basketball. Playing basketball in jail took about as much getting used to as the language. At first, after crashing into people, or elbowing them, I'd apologize profusely. So naturally, I got some looks. And when I would stand under the basket, I'd get shoved out by someone's backside. The only remedy for that was to shove them back. They seem to like that, and I feel I've earned a certain amount of respect on the court. And jail, being so petty, a little of anything and your "livin' large."

So, for all you first-time white boys visiting us for awhile, here's your official "White Man's Guide To Rikers Island."

Once you're in receiving — "the bullpen" — if you have any possessions — cigarettes, magazines, whatever — don't smoke them; sleep on them. You can wait until later. It's best to pretend you're asleep. This way, more goodies for me an' you later. If you see any white faces in there, go like peanut butter to jelly.

Step 1: Upon your first dormitory entry at One Upper. Look for the white section. There probably won't be one, but it's nice to dream. Avoid the back at all costs. Number one, if you have anything to give, they'll be asking for it. Number two, it's too noisy. People in the back only sleep when they're supposed to be awake, like when they're standing at attention being counted by the correction officer, or if it's time to go to work. At orientation, sign up for Work Release and Conditional Release. These programs usually go to crackheads, but maybe they'll make a mistake. I've been there, and it's the love boat, pal.

Step 2: Upon your next arrival at Six Lower, continue step 1.

Step 3: Your third stop should be a stay for several weeks. If you plan on buying plenty at the commissary, be sure to:

3a: Make friends with the biggest, meanest guy in there. You'd be surprised at the peace and serenity a few cigarettes and cookies will bring.

3b: Make friends with everyone in your general vicinity. It's best to store cookies and snacks in someone else's locker. Because when you go in your own for cookies, even the dead wake up. It's best to look like someone owes you. Offer them about one-fourth of your pack. Believe me, it's worth it.

Step 4: If you lose your money? Every inmate's nightmare. Have your costly lawyer on the outside threaten a class action lawsuit. Contact the Mayor's office. Have family picket City Hall and stop traffic. Encourage the entire dormitory to go on a hunger strike.

Step 5: If someone tries to sweat you — that is, encourage you to give him your possessions — usually a firm NO! will do. If not, move your bed in front for protection. As a last resort, use hand signal at throat: "THAT SHIT IS DEAD, MOTHERFUCKER." When saying this, try to look as psychotic as possible. I suggest shaving your head before trying this, for cosmetic purposes. Tattoos are excellent sweat preventers.

If all of the above fail, have your lawyer on the

outside get you Protective Custody, recommended for anyone under 4'5", under 110 pounds. If you don't mind being with the homos, this may be for you.

Step 6: Find out who the head Juggler is. If he's down on his luck, he may need an investor. One carton will get you two. Split the profits and you'll be parlaying in your dorm.

6a: Always juggle something. It's fun and keeps you busy going from locker to locker.

Step 7: Sports. You'll find any sport you play here, half the time will be lost on arguments.

7a: Softball. Choose a position where the ball never goes. The mitts are for hardball — too small and soft to catch anything. Don't go for home runs. The ball is dead and only will go so far. Just hit the ball anywhere. They'll drop it anyway. And you'll win friends and respect in the Puerto Rican community, who make up most of the baseball players. Be sure to argue over any call, even if it's an outright lie. The bigger the lie, the better. Loudest man wins.

7b: Basketball. I know, we can't jump, but some of us are tall, so there. Don't dribble; it will be stolen. When under the basket, box them out strong. If you don't move them, they'll move you out. Fight back under the boards. You will find a new sense of freedom and respect among the brothers. You may even not get picked last. Don't take any long shots. If you miss, you'll never hear the end of it. Pass a lot. Your teammates will appreciate it. After smashing into someone or elbowing them in the eye, don't apologize. Just say, "You know I didn't mean that. You okay?" And hustle your butt off. Even if you suck, everybody loves someone who tries hard.

Any questions?

The Night Was Clear and Cold
From *Sounding Brass*
by Marsh Cassady

All these years, Frank, you wondered why I never
mentioned my folks. Well, they never wanted me. I was
an unwelcome intruder, stealing pieces of their lives. I
remember one time when I was a little kid, my mother
accused me of trying to kill her by being born, and of
ruining her career as a musician. "Every time I tried to
practice, you cried," she said. "You were a selfish little
boy." And another time, when I was no more than three
or four, she packed her suitcase and said she was
leaving and not coming back. I was such a horrible
child, she said, that I didn't deserve a mother. She left,
and I was all alone with no one to care how hard I cried.

I wasn't allowed to call them Mom and Dad. They
were Helen and Dan to me and everyone else. You know,
he was just as bad as she was, maybe even worse.
When I was seventeen, just before Christmas my senior
year in high school, my grandparents came for a visit.
Grandpa and I were sitting at the kitchen table talking
about some evangelist or other — Billy Graham, I think.
Anyhow, I said he was rich and should use all that
money to help the poor. Grandpa disagreed, and I asked
him to explain what he meant. Dan was sitting in a
chair up against the wall off to one side, repairing a
toaster or something. He told me to stop arguing, and I
said we weren't, we were just talking. I turned back and
started to say something else to Grandpa. Dan jumped
up and grabbed my arm and dragged me into the dining
room.

He was a powerful man — a good three inches
shorter than I was, still he outweighed me. I tried to
struggle free, but he slammed me into a corner, grabbed
me around the neck and began to squeeze. At the same

time, he pounded my head — crack! crack! crack! — against the wall. Stop, I thought, oh God, please stop! He'd hurt me before, but never like this. My vision began to go like a gate being shut across my eyes, starting at the periphery and swinging in toward the center. I grabbed Dan's wrists and tried to pry his hands from around my neck. He only squeezed harder. Helen was upstairs making up a bed for Grandma and Grandpa and must have heard the commotion. She came tearing down and into the dining room. "Dan!" she screamed, running toward him and grabbing his arm. "Stop, for God's sake, stop! You're going to kill him." He released me then and stepped back. I staggered forward and caught my balance. I felt like my throat was crushed, and there was this ring of white hot fire around my neck. I raced to the kitchen, grabbed my coat from a hook by the door, and stumbled outside and down the steps of the porch.

The night was clear and cold. I was supposed to go caroling in Clivesville. I zipped up my jacket, ran down Second and turned up the hill. By the time I got to Sixth, I had the worst headache of my life, so bad it was making me ill. I slowed to a walk. I knew my father was frustrated. I knew money was scarce. Most of the kids who took music lessons had quit, because their parents couldn't afford to pay him. But that wasn't my fault, damn it. My dad didn't need to take it out on me.

Anyhow, as I was thinking these things, I stopped for a moment, aware of the utter silence. No sound at all, not even the barking of a dog. I started trudging on again, the frozen blades of grass at the side of the road breaking under my feet like glass. I knew I couldn't go caroling now, but I kept on walking toward Clivesville. My jacket had a fur collar — an aviator's jacket, maroon in color — and that soft fur rubbed my neck so bad I could hardly stand it. I unzipped the jacket and took it off. So what if I got sick? The wind whipped through the neck of my shirt like icy water rolling down my back. What was I going to do when I got to Clivesville? I thought. What did it matter? Nobody cared. I wasn't sure I cared myself. I thought, my father always treats me like shit, my mother, too. So maybe I am shit.

Then I thought maybe I'd freeze to death and that would be that. Or I'd get hit by a car. Maybe I'd try to help things along. I fluffed my jacket into a pillow and laid it on the white center line of that macadam road, old Route 30, the Lincoln Highway. So I lay down, my head in the middle of the jacket, and drew my legs up to my chest and closed my eyes. I figured if I were lucky, it would all end quickly. But nothing happened. After awhile, I opened my eyes. My breath hung in the air like a trail of ghostly balloons. Occasionally, a leaf blew by, or I heard a far-off car horn. I began to shake. The running and the walking had made me sweat, and the sweat was beginning to freeze.

Time passed as in a dream, and I don't know how long I lay there. For the first time, ever or since, I'll bet, that damned road stayed empty, and I got tired of waiting to die. I sat up and looked off in the distance at the trees making stark silhouettes against the light of the moon and the stars twinkling hundreds of light-years away, some maybe even dead, but their light still streaming down. So anyhow, I stood up, put on my jacket and kept on walking.

Pretty soon I got to Clivesville and went to see Thelma and Dick Polsky. They used to live next door. Dick was at the VFW, and Thelma wouldn't believe me when I told her what had happened. So I gulped this glass of water she handed me and stumbled outside. I'd walked eleven miles already, and it was late. So what do you think, Frank? Would I have let a car run over me if one had come along? I didn't know then, and I don't know now. But I seriously doubt I would have. I never really wanted to die . . . did I? Sometimes I had trouble knowing what was real and what was only my imagination. I was just a kid. Seventeen years old. So I hiked back home.

Vietnam and Later
by Armand A. Ruhlman III

Those kids were like vicious insects. Thousands of them. Crawling in the dust. Waiting for us. Crawling all over the jeep. Grabbing at us. Grabbing at anything they could take. Fighting each other for a piece of nothing. Every crumb, every scrap of garbage. It was all gone. In the blink of an eye. Then they started pawing at us, trying to rip the clothes off our backs. Trying to take anything. Something. Whatever could help them stay alive for another few hours. Something to eat, sell, steal, cook, trade, sleep on, live in, die with. We started beating them back. To get them off the jeep. To let us leave. Kicking them, punching them, cracking their faces with our M-16's. They were cursing us, scratching at us. Trying to gnaw at us with their teeth. The little bastards started biting us. Biting me. Trying to sink their nasty little teeth into my bones. No shit. Their tiny, little teeth. Hungry teeth. Desperate teeth. They didn't just want food. They wanted blood. It's funny. They were like insects. We were like cattle. Cattle in a cattle car. Cattle in combat boots. Robots in army green. Waiting for a trip to nowhere to start. A free fall into a thousand horrors. One year to go. Minus 5 minutes.

Roaches. These kids were collecting roaches. Can you believe that? To eat. Yeah. To cook and eat. Well, I don't know if they actually bothered to cook the damn things. But they were crawling through the gutter. These kids with their baggy of roaches. Swear to God. Just down the block from the b-girls on Tudo Street. No relation to Bourbon Street. No way. No jazz. No music. No strippers. But lots of b-girls. Friendly b-girls. Too friendly. Too hungry for a tip. Tip, shit. They wanted to pick your pockets dry. Bone dry. The hate was always there. Right beneath the smiles. Right on the edge of their sticky fingertips. I don't blame 'em. None of them.

Hell, man, I'd be pissed, too, if somebody was trying to kill me with every kind of device modern science could produce. From Zippo lighters to carpet bombing. Yessiree. I'd be real pissed. I'd hate you. I'd want to kill you. Kill you with my eyes. Kill you with my teeth. Kill you before you killed me. Piss on the cold war. A hot, dirty, slimy, stinking, nothing little country in the middle of nowhere. That's all I remember. And trees. They had lots of trees. The French were big on trees, I guess. But the French were gone. The sidewalks were filled with crippled beggars throwing their bodies in front of you. Mothers carrying deformed children in baskets. Twisted, warped things. Hustlers selling army issue T-bone steaks. Pimps. Drug dealers. Hookers. Rich, poor. Sick, well. Well, nothing was ever really well in that place.

There was this lifer in the office. Guy named Wilson. Total lifer pig. Hated cherries like me. Hated draftees. Hated anybody who wasn't gung ho. He was always telling me he'd send me to the field if I didn't get on the stick.

"Get with it, Murphy. Get your cherry ass in gear. Don't be such a limp dick in the wind. Start typing, man. Do those reports. Do 'em like your life depended on it. 'Cause it does, pal. You wouldn't last two seconds out there in the bush, Murphy. You'd probably drop your weapon and run. You'd piss in your pants and crawl on the ground crying for your momma. You'd beg to come back here. To good old sarge. You'd say anything, do anything to get out of it. This is a picnic, Murphy, what you've got here.

I did have it easy where I was, except for pulling guard on the perimeter at night, all night. I hated being out there, every second of it. Me and an M-60 machine gun that could blow you to hell and back.

I was always edgy looking out into the dark, always

thinking maybe the VC were right out there, just far enough away in the darkness so I couldn't see 'em. My first time out there, I thought they were going to come up through the floor of the bunker and slit my throat open. Get me while I was groggy, while I was starting to slip off. Then something would happen, some rush, some fear thing would shoot through me. I'd see things. Hear things. Stuff would start to happen. Faces. Bodies. Like a movie screen in front of me. Like some movie was playing right out there on the perimeter. My own personal movie in hell. But then I'd see her. My calendar girl. She was great. She was gorgeous. She'd blow kisses at me, smile at me, make me forget about the hateful eyes, the hateful teeth. She'd take me on a magic carpet ride across her skin, against her lips.

"You got to pull together, Murphy, got it? It's a group thing, man, especially out there in the bush. You try to mess over some dude who's counting on you, hell, you're dead meat. Our people will blow you away in a second, less than a second, if you get in their way. If you can't be on the team. It happens, pal. Pussy dudes like you get shot all the time. Shot. Fragged. Gotten rid of. Somehow. Some way. Believe it. Cats who are into their own thing, they never make it back, except in a body bag. Don't even last a day out there."

So, that's what I did. I got out. Alive. I deserted. I made it out of there. That's what I did. I made it out of there. I know I made it out of there, because here I am back in the living room. I don't know whose living room but I'm back in a living room. I made it home. Except it's not home anymore. It stopped being home a long time ago. Way before I left. Before I ran away. All it was, was a dark, empty living room with people who kept telling me lies. Lies that I was their son and they loved me. But they didn't seem to know what love was. Or know how to love. They just wanted to sit on the sofa, pretend everything would be okay. Just sit there and wait to die. Unless, of course, you were already dead.

I had to change my name. In case they came after me. For leaving early. For deserting. That's what they call it. I call it finding a way to live before I die. I like my new name. It's fun. It's adventurous. Quite challenging to be The Wizard. The Wizard, protecting the Crystal City. Come in, Crystal City. This is The Wizard. Do you read me? Transmission of Martian memo has been intercepted. Repeat. Memo from Mars has been intercepted and decoded as follows: Alien star fleet is quickly approaching our atmosphere with an assault force of unknown capability. They have issued the following ultimatum to Earth: Oh, does eat oats and goats jump moats and little lambs eat ivy. Diddly diddie do, wouldn't you? This is The Wizard. Over and out. Yeah, man, way out.

My Father
by John Hallow

My earliest recollection of my father is that of a man who I seldom saw or spoke to. He worked long hours on his feet, six days a week, and when he was home, he read the newspaper, listened to the radio and went to bed early. As I grew older, on the occasional Sunday, he would take me to the theatre, which was his great love.

He had immigrated to this country from Russia just prior to World War I. He became a barber and worked the next couple of decades in the Rialto Barber Shop, located in the basement of the Times Building on Times Square. Working right in the heart of the theatre district, many of his customers were vaudevillians, actors, stagehands and the like.

We lived in the Bronx, so he had to take the train to and from work. And working right next to the subway, he was aware of the constant din. All this finally took its toll on him, when he developed a fear of not only riding the subway, but of tunnels and bridges as well. To this day I can see the panic on his face when I accompanied him on the train while he made one last effort to overcome his fear. He never conquered it and opened a small barber shop in the Bronx, which he could reach by trolley car.

In 1943, I was drafted and my parents moved to Lakewood, New Jersey, where my father worked in the barber shop of one of the large hotels, never again to return to New York. Not being able to go through a tunnel or over a bridge, I still don't know how he got to New Jersey. I have asked him about this, but he seems to have blocked it out of his memory.

When I got out of the Army Air Corps at the end of World War II, I decided that I would become an actor. My father strongly disapproved, since I had already trained to be a commercial artist, was talented and could in all probability find a job immediately. Becoming an actor meant going to school days and working nights and weekends, and then starting a life of struggle, rejection and uncertainty. As it turned out, I was fortunate to become a "working actor," which means you haven't achieved fame or fortune, but you manage to make a very nice living working at your craft without having to supplement your income by working at a "civilian" job.

Whenever I was in a Broadway show or working in the area, my mother would come to see me perform. But since my father could not make the trip, he never saw me on stage. He had to be content with seeing me in commercials or the occasional TV stint. He never voiced his feelings to me, but my mother told me he would inform the whole neighborhood that his son was going to be on TV, however small the part.

In 1980, I got a job at the Paper Mill Playhouse in Millburn, New Jersey, playing the part of Herbie in *Gypsy*. Herbie's a wonderful part, because it's not only a great acting role, it also gives you the opportunity to sing and dance. And I was playing opposite the fabulous Dolores Gray. A friend of my father's told him that since Millburn was not that far away from Lakewood, he would drive him there. By now, my mother had passed on. I was elated that my father was finally going to see me on stage, and in such a wonderful part in such a wonderful show.

After the show, I wondered that my father had not come backstage and went looking for him. I found him standing all alone on stage, with the work light the only illumination. A small, frail man, he took me in his arms, and for the first time in his life, he said, "I love you, son." And for the first time in my life, I replied, "I love you, Daddy."

My father, who is now 95, has never seen me on stage again. But we do say "I love you" a lot.

About the Editor

For twenty-nine years, Catherine Gaffigan has worked in theatre, television and film as director, producer, actress and teacher. As an actress, she made her New York debut opposite Dustin Hoffman in *Journey of the Fifth Horse*. She toured the country for two years in *Cabaret*, played Lady MacBeth, did stints in summer and winter stock, made many television commercials, suffered the agonies of soap opera life, and appeared in both Broadway versions of *Whose Life Is It, Anyway?* Her films include *Julia* and Brian DePalma's thriller *Sisters*. Since 1971, she has taught Master Classes in Acting in her own New York studio. In 1987, she produced and directed the North American premiere of *Lady Susan*, based on the Jane Austen novel, for the Jane Austen Society. She subsequently directed *Deals and Deceptions, Restaurant Romances, An Evening of Hilarity and Hidden Agendas, The J.A.R.* (world premiere), *Dance Me to the End of Love*, and *Tom and Viv*. Catherine holds a BA in English from St. John's University and an MFA in Drama from The Catholic University of America. She also trained in the New York studio of James Tuttle.